THE THORN

THE THORN

Seven Surprising Effects of Suffering and Temptation

DEVIN SCHADT

Excerpts from the English translation of the
Catechism of the Catholic Church, Second Edition,
©1994, 1997, 2000 by Libreria Editrice Vaticana,
United States Catholic Conference, Washington, D.C.
All rights reserved.

Unless otherwise noted,
Scripture quotations are from
the Douay-Rheims version of Sacred Scripture.
Copyright 1914 by John Murphy Company

Cover Design: Devin Schadt

© 2020 by Devin Schadt
All right reserved.

ISBN: 978-1-7327739-8-1
Printed in the United States.

Stewardship: A Mission of Faith
11 BlackHawk Lane
Elizabethtown, PA 17022
StewardshipMission.org

Contents

Why It Won't Go Away **9**

Effect #1:

Reliance on God **27**

Effect #2:

Patience **43**

Effect #3:

Perseverance **59**

Effect #4:

Mercy **71**

Effect #5:

Humility **79**

Effect #6:

Gratefulness **91**

Effect #7:

Knowledge of God **99**

Why It Won't Go Away

I can't stop it. I wish it would go away. Why do I keep doing this–even though, deep down, I don't want to do it? How do I break free? Why can't God heal me of it? Does He even care? Does He even exist?

Have you, in your darkest and most private moments, voiced something similar? Do you suffer from a haunting temptation? a re-occurring tendency toward the same sin? a problematic habit? a debilitating addiction that relentlessly pursues you, enticing you?

We all suffer from it. Not one of us is excluded. All of us have that one thing that plagues us, drags us down, and never seems to be removed completely. Just when we think that we have miraculously subdued it and that victory is ours, the scourge resurfaces, emerging with ever greater force.

When I address crowds of men, I ask a probing question: Who here suffers from a haunting temptation, a physical impediment, an infernal sin, a thorn that has yet to be removed? There isn't a man who doesn't raise his hand or nod his head. All of us have a thorn, or multiple thorns, that prick at our pride. The fact is: you are not alone.

But even if misery loves company, that idea offers very little consolation. It really isn't much of a consolation to be with a community of people in hell if you're in hell, regardless of how much you enjoy the company. The thorn remains, and the fact that we all suffer from its relentless sting doesn't lessen the pain.

For those of us who believe in God and His power to heal and redeem us, who have made that dangerous leap of becoming vulnerable enough to expose the wound to Him and admit our personal failures, who dared to trust that God would intervene—we often feel abandoned and betrayed when that divine intervention and healing does not come. We are tempted to believe that either God doesn't exist, or He doesn't love me.

We are like toddlers who, coaxed by mommy to walk, dared a few awkward, uncoordinated steps, and then wondered why we weren't any closer to those secure hands awaiting us. Toddlers fall, and sometimes they fall hard. And sometimes mommies let them.

The Thorn

But somewhere in a toddler's forming intellect he processes the event and wonders, "Why did you pull back? I trust you with all my heart. Why did you let me fall?" Mommy replies: "Because by letting you fall, you learn to walk."

It appears to be a dirty trick, breaking the rules of the game. It's cheating to propose a target to someone and then suddenly move it when he has nearly attained it.

Likewise, it appears unjust, if not cruel, to coach a sprinter to train for a 400-meter sprint, but because the runner for the 800 meter event became injured, the coach slots him for the 800 meter event. The runner establishes his pace based on the pre-determined distance. When that distance is suddenly extended, he realizes that he may not have the stamina to keep his pace, or even complete the race. But he doesn't know if he doesn't try.

Why It Won't Go Away

Yet, we know from experience that when the rules of the game change, we adapt, we increase our skill set, or we give up.

The competitive marksman learns to shoot at live targets with erratic movement patterns. If he perseveres in his practice, he eventually becomes a skilled sharpshooter. The sprinter whose finish line is unexpectedly extended trains harder and wiser, learning to maintain the balance between having a reserve with pushing his physical limits. The toddler who is allowed to fall eventually learns to walk and then run.

In all of these situations there is one constant: the person must keep at it, and never give up. In Christian language: he must not lose faith.

Observing any of these examples from the outside, it is easy to understand the principle at work: the skateboarder's scabbed knees, the untrained martial artist's lack of endurance, the hunter's failure to bag the elusive ten pointer. If they keep at it, they will eventually become more proficient. If they desire to succeed, they will fail and fall—and at times in the most ugly and humiliating ways—but they will also need to courageously rise from such personal defeats before they actually succeed. Every failure increases our capacity for real success. As the saying goes, "Success is going from one failure to another with great enthusiasm."

Yet, when we attempt to observe our own personal plight from the "inside," we have difficulty perceiving that principle at work. Rather, we are overwhelmed by the oppressive weight of hopelessness induced by our personal failures and are gravely tempted to believe that there is no point in battling to overcome our shortcomings. It's easier to just forget about the fight and give in. We hear the pathetic mantra circulating in our self-defeated one-track mind: "You can't change it, anyway. You might as well accept it and enjoy life."

But is that true? Even if *you* can't change "it," does caving in and ceasing to better yourself make life enjoyable?

During such dark seasons, we pray, fervently imploring God–even with tears–to remove the thorn. We come to the conclusion, however, that God isn't listening. "Is God against me?" "Why doesn't He care?" "Grace, healing, redemption is a big pile of --------." "Jesus is a lie." "And come to think of it, I've never heard God's voice, seen any evidence of Him, or ever witnessed a real-deal miracle."

Instead of going down that path, it may be more beneficial to ask, "Why would God allow this thorn to exist and persist?"

Maybe God *is* listening. Maybe God *isn't* against you. Maybe God *does* care. Actually, there is no maybe about it! He is listening, and does care for you, and your thorn is proof of His love. How can that be? How can something that seems so ungodly lead a person to God?

Let's consider the question, "What if the thing that appears to be a curse is actually a blessing?" "What if what appears to separate you from God is actually intended by God to draw you closer to Him?" We flee a shoreline with pointed, cutting stones to dive into a vast ocean, swimming against the tide, believing that we will eventually arrive at freedom's unseen, promised shore of liberation despite our inability to conquer ourselves. But the journey becomes too much. Exhausted and breathless, we become motionless. There's nothing more to do but sink. Then, suddenly, the waves sweep us up, returning us to the shore we fled.

Sometimes we become lost in the sea of self-will, self-mastery, and self-conquering. We eventually realize that, humanly speaking, we simply don't have what it takes to overcome sin, temptation, and evil. We set out to flee from the thorn, symbolized by that rocky sharp beach, hoping to leave it permanently behind, thinking that is what God wants. Yet, the farther we get from shore, the farther we are from God and his will.

Often the waters that take us away from God are intended to draw us back to Him. Sometimes the curse of the thorn is actually God's blessing. Often the failures surrounding your particularly haunting weakness will–if you stay the course–increase your capacity for union with God.

How can this be? The idea is counterintuitive. Clearly, I am in no way advocating sin. We must do all in our power to overcome temptation, and not let the temptation overcome us with despair. But what do we do when we've seemingly exhausted "all in *our* power" to overcome our weakness?

We are all familiar with that disconsolate feeling that overcomes us after we've fallen. The devil seems to rub our nose in our sinful poop, convincing us that we're failures: "You've done it yet again. How could God ever forgive you? You promised Him that you'd never do this terrible thing again. Now look at you. You're pathetic. You can't go back to Him. You're a traitor–no better than Judas."

God, however, has a different message for you–a word of hope. St. Paul said, "And lest the greatness of the revelations should exalt me, there was given me a thorn in my flesh, an angel of Satan, to buffet me. For which thing thrice I besought the Lord, that it might depart from me. And [God] said to me: My grace is sufficient for thee; for power is made perfect in weakness. Gladly therefore will I glory in my infirmities [weakness] that the power of Christ may dwell in me" (2 Cor 2:12).

God is not as concerned about the sin as much as the sinner. God isn't merely concerned about you "not sinning." He wants you to be a saint. Avoiding sin is not the same as union with God (although it is needed to be in union with God). The Gospels recount many men who fulfilled the Law, yet their hearts were far from God. Often, when living a good, moral life, free of mortal sin, we begin to assume that we are sufficient unto ourselves, that we are doing well, that we are morally strong–even exalted. Yet, that is precisely when our personal "goodness" can become an evil; our strength can become a blind, debilitating, weakness. We begin to believe that we are unlike others, that we have risen above "those sins." Consequently, we fall into the most heinous sin of all: pride. That is why your thorn is so essential: to help you refrain from exalting yourself.

If you produce good fruit, such seeds of pride might become thorns and thistles that will choke and kill its growth. Often we are quite unaware of a sinful attachment that, like mold, grows and metastasizes in the dark crevices of the soul.

This insidious cancer is difficult for us to identify because we have lived with it nearly our entire life, and our familiarity with it makes us blind to it. God permits the thorn for the purpose of uprooting the deeper vice–the one that we cannot perceive, because the vice that we cannot perceive is our most insidious enemy.

God is not as concerned with us "being good" as He is with us obtaining the ultimate good. We can appear to be good, but lack the ultimate good. Therefore, He often allows a thorn to help us understand that we are not good in ourselves, but need God, the ultimate good. We need Him to shine His eternal, merciful light into the dark places of our soul, to help us discover those things that are keeping us from Him and, inversely, those things that will help unite us to Him.

We can sometimes hyper-focus on what we are doing–good or bad–and miss completely what God is doing in us. It is ironic that when we think that we are "doing good," God may not be doing much in us. When we feel strong we can forget our weakness; and this moral amnesia, which is a lack of humility, deflects God's grace. God says: "My strength is made perfect in your weakness." When we forget to acknowledge our weakness, we neglect to depend upon His strength.

My previous home did not have a garage. Iowa winters can be brutal. Each winter morning, I was faced with the high probability of scraping my windshield.

The Thorn

Scrapers would snap, credit cards would bend. Running late for an appointment, I'd scrape the bare minimum, attempting to see the road through a small clearing. The days that the ice was thin or non-existent, I would thank God. The days when it was thick, my scraper was broke, and I was running late, I would remember God, thanking Him for those days when the ice wasn't as bad–and perhaps ask him for more days like that.

Now that I own a home with a garage, I am not as concerned about the weather or my windshield. And honestly, the practice of thanking God for not having to scrape my windshield has faded. Now that my windshield is ice-free, I should thank God every winter morning for this gift. But I have forgotten to thank God, because I have forgotten the ice and the difficulty it caused.

Iowa winter weather combined with having no garage constituted a "thorn" that reminded me of my relationship with and dependence upon God. But now that the thorn is absent, I'm not reminded as often of my dependence and need for God. When the thorn is removed, we often think of God less.

Sometimes a personal struggle exists for the purpose of deepening your relationship with God. Whether your "thorn" is a physical limitation, a sexual temptation, financial hardship, difficulties with employment, negative thoughts, depression, anxiety, hormonal disorders, fatigue, compulsive shopping, feelings of guilt or scrupulosity, a haunting past, addiction to food, stretching the truth, a tendency toward envy or jealousy, the urge to speak ill about others, desiring to be the center of attention, being repulsed by human beings, an inability to lose those love handles, lack of patience, inability to persevere, inability to fast due to physical limitations, being seduced by internet ads, addiction to your smart phone,

The Thorn

a string of broken relationships, chocolate, the inability to make real and lasting friendships, same sex attraction, judging and condemning others, fear of failure, lust, substance or alcohol abuse, a disordered desire to avoid conflict, overcoming self-importance, inability to perform sexually, deep seated pride, self-indulgence—whether you have a thorn or a thorn *bush*, God promises you that it is not arbitrary but has a divine purpose.

Your thorn exists so that you will learn to rely not on your limited self, but rather on our unlimited God. Trust is the foundation of every true, lasting relationship. A relationship without trust is unsustainable. God permits the thorn to help you learn to trust Him; and in trusting Him, you become trustworthy.

Whatever your weakness is, God has allowed that weakness to remain in you so that you will learn to remain in him.

Why It Won't Go Away

This little book is unique because it will not be focusing on a particular temptation or tendency toward sin, but rather on why God permits the thorn and the potential for that mysterious healing He grants by means of the thorn.

Perhaps, like St. Paul you've sought the Lord, begging for your thorn to depart from you–and yet, to this day, it remains. God promises you that His power will be perfected–not in your strength to do good, but in your weakness.

Whatever your weakness is, regardless of the nature of your thorn, it exists to ensure that God's power may dwell in you. Your thorn, if understood and embraced properly, will have seven amazing, grace-filled effects that will allow God's power to be manifest in you. It is my hope that this little work will help you–like St. Paul–learn to be thankful and

The Thorn

glorify God for your thorn(s) so that the power of Christ may dwell in you.

Effect #1:

Reliance on God

Most children spend their formative years living at home yet wishing that they lived on their own. The idea of working for oneself–rather than for another–is universally appealing. How many times have we heard someone say, "I can do it myself." Our culture, particularly in America, idealizes if not idolizes rugged individualistic autonomy.

The Thorn

The self-reliant individual used to be synonymous with the American dream: to live on your own; to own your own land; to have your own house; to have your own revenue generator; to be your own man–without owing anything to anyone. We often equate self-sufficiency with autonomy, autonomy with freedom, and freedom with happiness.

We admire individuals whose skill-set, talents, and abilities enable them to "get the job done" and "get it done right." The man who built his own home; the person who rewired his own electrical; the at-home mechanic who changes his car's oil; the individual who crafts five star cuisine from a handful of ingredients; the seamstress who designs and makes her own clothing; the do-it-yourself-er who pours his own concrete driveway. They get the job done, and get it done right, all without outsourcing the project to someone else–without shelling out their hard-earned cash.

Additionally, many of us have experienced the massive frustration that results from depending on someone who doesn't come through for us: the tile guy who takes his down payment, spends a half day prepping the site, and leaves never to return. Your sub-contractor misses your deadline–for the third time–convincing your client that you are completely irresponsible and unreliable. The employee who called in sick two weeks ago with a head cold, last week had to skip work due to a death in the family, and this week left a message saying that his car won't start and he won't be coming in. The dad who continues to promise he'd be there for his child's game but always has to work late. Nobody respects a person who consistently fails at delivering, at following through.

We've learned all to well the lesson that "people disappoint people." It has been said that if you depend on anyone, you will inevitably learn to depend on no one. If you depend on someone you will inevitably, eventually, be disappointed. It's an unwritten rule: people have failed us, are failing us, and will fail us.

When a person reaches full saturation of disappointment in people, he commits himself to determine ways to accomplish his goals himself. Which brings us to the heart of the issue: We don't want to be disappointed, let-down, used, or taken advantage of by another because of his failings. To avoid this, we strive to be self-sufficient, self-reliant, secure in ourselves. We condition ourselves not to depend on others.

Even though the man who builds his own house appears autonomous, nevertheless he purchased the framing package from a lumber yard, the shingles from a roofing resource, and he didn't melt sand to make the panes for his soundproof windows. At the most fundamental level, he did not create the land upon which his house stands. The truth is that he is dependent on others, and without them the completion of the project is impossible.

A person may pride himself that he doesn't have to swing by the local coffee shop for a fine cup of java because he grinds his own coffee beans, boils his own water, steeps his own grounds, and presses his own cup of brew. From where and from whom did he acquire the beans? Who manufactured the grinder? Which municipality piped water into his home? The point is that in every aspect of our lives, we depend on someone else for something. A person may have the freedom of going on vacation, but he's dependent on the manufacturer who made his automobile and the oil industry who fuels it, because without them his vacation becomes a stay-cation.

Which brings us to another important point: most of the time, the people we depend upon don't actually fail us. The coffee shop is almost always open; the gas pumps almost always pump gas; the school is open on school days, save an occasional snow day (whether our children are happy about that or not); The city busses are usually on time; the subway transports commuters daily; your internet provider connects your smart phone to the world constantly; a dispatcher immediately picks up the phone when you dial 911. This point is further validated by our initial reaction when there is an interruption in our electric service. Put mildly, we freak out. People don't panic and become upset about things that are common, normal, and expected. They become alarmed when the unexpected, the inconvenient, and the abnormal occur.

Corporations, cooperatives, and companies all function consistently because they collaborate–which

Reliance on God

is another way to say that people depend upon other people to achieve a common goal.

I may believe that I am free to drive anywhere, but that would not be possible if the local, state, and national governments did not build the highway systems and maintain them. We depend on people who depend on people, who together make things work together.

Dependence on others is not only a matter of pragmatic order, but also is an expression of beauty.

A solo fiddler can be entertaining, but a symphony's robust string section is elevating. The all-pro fullback may be the MVP, but if he alone had to contend with his opponents' defensive eleven, he'd lose every time. A single mountain is beautiful, but nothing compared to a range of them. Colorado is a great state, but its land is a part of a majestic nation of purple mountains' majesty and amber waves of grain. A single thread may have a certain delicate beauty, but it is overlooked and swept in the trash unless it becomes woven into a greater tapestry. A half of a pound of beef is fine, but with bacon, tomato, cheese, ketchup, and the right seasoning, sandwiched between two brioche buns, it moves from being a slab of beef to being a burger.

The human person intuitively admires those finely tuned mechanisms comprised of a multitude of moving parts, seamlessly collaborating and coordinating to form a single complete entity. Whether it is a computer or an orchestra, a film comprising producers, artists, set designers and the like, or a Rueben sandwich: we relish the final, completed product that is composed of many parts. And we should, because there is a glorious and nearly transcendent, unspeakable, indescribable character to things that demand precise harmony. Harmony is the beauty obtained when people use order to collaborate and anticipate one another for the purpose of composing something unified.

Even though we know the most successful enterprises are collaborations, harmonies if you will, nevertheless, we continue to idealize and idolize self-reliance. To rely on yourself without collaborating with others or to allow others to rely on your unreliability is to do harm to the harmony of humanity.

There is a similar dynamic at work in our relationship with God. We don't want to be too reliant on God because, frankly, He has been known to disappoint us. A man seeks God in hopes of a promotion and an increase in salary, but is overlooked while his co-worker receives the promotion. A woman desperately prayed to be healed from cancer and now has only months to live. The couple who didn't demand which sex their child would be, but prayed only for a healthy baby, were given a child with downs syndrome.

When things like these occur, we think, "God can't be trusted. He is unreliable. He disappoints."

Upon deeper, more thoughtful reflection, we realize that He could say the same thing about us–and He would be right. "I asked you to save yourself for marriage, but you slept around." "I gave you that financial windfall, and you went back on your promise to tithe and help those starving kids in Africa." "You said that if your wife would come back to you, you would give up the pornography, but you didn't."

Remember the tragic shock that occurred on 9/11– the terrorist attack on American soil that sent a thunderbolt through the nation's heart? The days following that horrific tragedy, churches were full of penitents on bended knee, imploring the Lord's mercy. Where are we today? Churches are emptier than ever, and perhaps so are our souls. No, we are not reliable.

Reliance on God

Nevertheless, God continues to share His benefits lavishly. Among the greatest of these gifts is to actually participate with Him in sharing His Gospel, in "saving" souls. Despite our sinfulness and lack of reliability, He allows us a place in the mission; He keeps us on His roster. Though we've failed Him on numerous occasions, He continues to encourage us to rise, beat the dirt from our knees, and help those who may not be as fortunate as us.

The sting of your thorn may persist and exist because you have yet to learn to be reliant upon God. Perhaps you rely too much on your own ways, experience, and knowledge. Perhaps, you like to do things yourself and avoid working with others. Ironically, the God who needs no one has decided to rely on you, but wants you to rely on Him to experience His love to the full.

If we are honest, it is difficult to trust God. Why? What child trusts a parent who causes him pain? We don't trust anyone who causes us pain. We keep such individuals at a distance and are guarded in their company. We simply don't want to be hurt again.

What father, if he is truly good, desires to inflict pain upon his child? Such a father would be monstrous. A true parent does not want his child to suffer or be the cause of his child's suffering. A true parent loves his child, and–this is the key–love desires the perfection of the other. Discipline develops that perfection, and discipline causes pain. Pain in this way leads us to perfection. The older generations used to say that the pain 'smarts' because the suffering caused by the pain reminds us to remember not to do that which causes us unnecessary pain–it makes us smart. The pain of discipline can help to make us smart, and eventually perfect.

Discipline without love, however, is tyranny; and love without discipline is child abuse. Both love and discipline are necessary. It is easy to forget that God does not cause suffering: sin and that evil causes disorder, which in turn cause suffering. This suffering is permitted as a way to perfect us. God draws us from disorder to order through love and discipline. He disciplines with love and loves with discipline.

The pain that we often experience in our relationship with God is born from His desire to perfect us. We hate the pain, and therefore begin to hate God who allows it. We confuse the pain with an absence of love, when in fact, the pain is proof that He loves us and wants to perfect us.

This dynamic demands radical trust and reliance on God, rather than a dependence on ourselves and what we think we need or should have. God promises that He will provide for us. But will that provision be what I want? The real question is: should I want what God determines is not worth wanting? Should I desire that which will harm me?

God sometimes responds to our requests with what appears to be "No." When He does, it pains us. But God is saying "yes" to harmony with Him, and "no" to what will harm our harmony. Often, we are too deeply attached to ourselves, what we want, and what we think is best for us. We are far too self-reliant.

The thorn exists to make us rely on the only One who can remove it. Our Lord tells us that only if you become like a little child will you enter the Kingdom of God. A child instinctively knows two things: first, I can't do everything myself; and second, my parents know what to do. We cannot do everything ourselves, and until we realize that fact, we are unable to truly rely on God who knows what to do for us, and also knows what is best for us.

Reliance on God

Your thorn exists to bring you to the conclusion, "God knows what is best for me. I don't." God allows the thorn to exist to help you to keep making the choice to no longer rely on your own disordered, self-serving ways, but to primarily rely upon Him.

The lesson that the child of God must learn, if the thorn is to ever be removed is: "Apart from [Jesus] you can do nothing." You can strategize and struggle, plot and plan, develop all sorts of coping mechanisms–but in the end, you cannot remove the thorn. And if you cannot remove the thorn, then self-reliance is not the answer. Your inability to remove your thorn helps you realize that you need to become reliant on the only One who can.

A confessor once said that self-reliance and self hatred are evil twin sisters. When you rely on yourself and accomplish something, you believe that you did

The Thorn

it yourself and are tempted to become prideful. When you rely on yourself and fail, you are tempted to hate yourself. If you dislike yourself or have self-hatred, it is a certain sign that you are too self-reliant and not reliant enough on God . . . and that is why your thorn remains: to help you realize this.

Reliance on God removes the sting of self-hatred. Children naturally and properly love themselves, because they are reliant and dependent upon their parents. They trust their parents–even when being disciplined. You and I are to become like little children who trust that the Heavenly Father will do what is absolutely best for us. The thorn exists and persists to help you realize how self-reliant you have become, while also summoning you to return to your Father and rely on Him.

Effect #2:

Patience

As I write this, I'm battling Influenza B; or rather, it's battling me. The chills, cold sweats, high fevers; congestion the consistency of molasses clogging my nose and trachea, relentless slow drip of mucus into my lungs, head splitting migraine, the impossibility of sleeping, difficulty breathing, dry eyes, and malaise–all make me believe that I'm dying.

The Thorn

I know; I'm pathetic. It's just a cold. I lie down but I cannot rest. I walk around like the living dead, with no where to go and no energy to get there. It's miserable. When will it end?

Isn't that the question we all ask while enduring something, anything disagreeable? We simply can't wait for it to be over. We're indignant that we are subjected to this type of torment. This is impatience.

Impatience has become a prevalent personality trait (disorder) among people living in the 21st century. Impatience can be viewed erroneously as a virtuous form of self-assertion or standing up for oneself, a form of holding people accountable for their failure to respond to our demands promptly.

We want it now. And why shouldn't we? We've been conditioned to believe that what we want now, we can have now. Technological advances, though good in themselves, have exacerbated this dynamic. Internet and cable providers appeal to us by boasting "on demand," "instant," "live streaming." Satellite technology combined with internet search engines and social media platforms grant us immediate access to nearly anything of interest. Whether the bank-line representative puts us on hold, we're sardined in miles of rush hour traffic, waiting in line at the fast food drive thru, choosing a check-out lane at the grocery store, waiting for a page on the internet to load–it is almost never fast enough for our liking.

We want instant results. "Lose 10 lbs in seven days." "Get your new body in less than a month." "Get your six-figure salary immediately upon graduating from college."

The Thorn

Ironically, the same man who condemns a recent college graduate for purchasing a home and an automobile that most senior account executives can't afford complains that he has seven more years until retirement. They both are guilty of the same vice: the college graduate wants the comfort and wealth of people twice his age without paying the dues of years of hard work, saving money, and experiential success. He signs the mammoth loan's terms and agreements, only to be haunted by the secret, stressful burden that he is a paycheck or two away from defaulting. He becomes possessed by his possessions because of his impatience. Whereas the man who "can't wait" to retire, is guilty of the same error. He simply wants to skip the remaining rungs on the ladder of labor and arrive at the top now.

We understand intuitively that there is a cost directly associated with impatience. Houses built from timber that were grown too fast weaken, warp, and eventually cost more to repair than to construct from scratch. If a person doesn't wait for his newly poured driveway to cure, but rather, parks his car on it before it hardens, he and his neighbors will always be reminded of his impatience.

Couple's who have sex on their first date later wonder why they have grown to hate the person whom they "loved" so passionately. They couldn't wait. They didn't patiently prepare for commitment.

It has been said that impatience is simply having unrealistic expectations. Which raises the question: what do we expect when we become impatient? Impatience demonstrates that we have a deep-seated pride, a form of self-entitlement. We subconsciously believe, "I deserve it now." Our impatience reveals that we perceive ourselves to be the central figure of the situations and circumstances around us. Often, we subconsciously believe ourselves to be the most important figure in the equation and that we ought to be treated as such.

Let that set in. When we are impatient, we are professing with our actions that we believe that we are the central figure in that situation. This indicates that we believe that we are the most important person and factor in that particular circumstance. This is a most unrealistic expectation. We simply can't expect others to believe that we are the central figure of importance in their lives. Why? Because others think the same as we do: they believe themselves to be the center of everything.

A young little leaguer who has yet to experience collegiate competition and has not developed the body mass, skill, and strength necessary to compete at that level, but believes that he ought to be playing pro-ball has unrealistic expectations. He is duped because he is too focused on himself and what he wants, rather than looking realistically at the world around him.

A thirteen-year-old girl who has not encountered the harsh sufferings and demands of life, cannot expect to write a best-selling novel that communicates life's most valuable lessons convincingly. We cannot teach what we have not learned. We can't lead unless first we learn to follow. Typically, after graduating third grade, the student doesn't apply for acceptance at a university.

To become skilled, accomplished, and respected for something, a person invests his time, effort, thought, and labor into achieving that something. This process of investing oneself demands a significant amount of trial and error: evaluating where and why we have erred; determining better solutions; testing the new solutions and comparing them with others; and then pushing for an even better solution. This demands patience. And we, as consumers, demand this patience from vendors.

Imagine yourself lying on a gurney awaiting surgical circumcision performed by a robot. You comment to the nursing staff about the technological advances of mankind and how amazing it is that a robot can actually perform surgery accurately. Then you begin to wonder how this machine was tested and ask out loud, "So how many years of research and testing went into this robot?" The doctor responds as he summons the anesthesiologist, "Oh, they didn't have enough time to test it to see if it actually works." The patient becomes the victim of impatience. And perhaps becomes a eunuch.

Regardless of what you want to achieve, doing it demands the patience to restrain yourself from short-circuiting the process.

Patience

This applies to even the most seemingly trivial aspects of life. For example, there is a tremendous difference between the quality of instant coffee and a French-pressed cup of java that is made from properly roasted beans, ground within moments of brewing the coffee, and steeped in hot water for at least five minutes. Steeping allows the freshly brewed coffee to become saturated with rich flavor, but it demands a little patience.

The Greek word for patience, *hupomoné* is a combination of the word *hypó*, which means "under," and *ménō*, which means "to remain." A person who is patient is willing to remain "under" whatever situation he is enduring for a greater, nobler good. Additionally, the Latin word for patience, *patientia* means to permit or bear suffering. The word "patient" as in "doctor-patient" is derived from this understanding.

The Thorn

The patient remains under the doctor's care, permitting the suffering that the physician's treatment inflicts, for the purpose of being healed. The virgin "remains under" her vow to be chaste for the greater good of her future husband.

The fact that we act impatiently demonstrates our unwillingness to remain in the situation, to permit the circumstances, or suffering. It is personal resistance to undertaking and accepting what it takes to be healed.

The person who honks his horn because the driver ahead of him hesitated a little too long before hitting the gas has not overcome the problem. He, in fact, demonstrates his problem. His irritated response indicates a deeper, personal problem that needs attention and healing.

Our acts of impatience are visible signs that we need to be healed of our pride, self-importance, and self-entitlement. Becoming irritated and annoyed in the trivial matters of life is a warning sign that we are making little spiritual progress, and if we are not progressing, we are digressing.

This brings us to a much deeper, fundamental challenge. Many Christians have an amazing ability to be patient—with everyone except themselves and their own spiritual progress. After years of prayer, works of charity, and asceticism, they wonder why they are not further along in their spiritual journey, why they are not as holy as they want to be. When faced with this self-analysis, they are tempted to grow impatient with themselves, become discouraged, and even despair and turn their backs on Christ–as if it were His fault. If impatience can be loosely defined as having unrealistic expectations, such a person unrealistically expects that he should be a saint already.

God, however, is not concerned with you feeling

good about yourself as much as he wants your self to be good. God wants us to learn valuable lessons, gain essential experience, be purified of disordered attachments (including our own self-perception and self-importance) in hopes that our transformation in Christ will be real and enduring.

We all suffer from spiritual cancer: vices, deep-seated tendencies toward sin. God is the divine physician who uses the scalpel of patience to cut out the cancer. This means that God will place us in situations that test and forge that patience. During such occasions, we are to remain "under the knife," permitting Him to heal us.

Impatience is not only a consequence of unrealistic expectations, but also a lack of respect and appreciation for an "exalted good." Patience not only helps us to focus on what we are expecting, but also the value of what we are hoping for.

Patience

A man who has just met a woman and works impatiently to get her into bed is failing to respect her "exalted good"; he doesn't appreciate her dignity. A person who is running late for work, exceeds the speed limit, and runs a red light fails to respect and honor the good of the other drivers' lives.

The man who blows up on a customer sales representative because of a lengthy hold time believes that his time is more important than her humanity.

Which brings us to another important point: One of the reasons we become impatient with our spiritual progress is that we don't respect the awesome grandeur of our salvation and sanctification in Christ. We have reduced it to something we can achieve on our own–like training and running for a marathon or as something that is freely distributed to everyone, like candy on Halloween. Yet, holiness, saintliness, and sanctification are tremendous gifts from God, exalted goods obtained by the exalted One who humbled himself to take on our sins and die on a cross so that we could be acceptable to God the Father. Yet the Christian, if he is to be like Christ, must follow Christ, who suffered patiently that we may also learn and receive His grace to be patient in our sufferings. It is vital that you and I learn to appreciate the exalted good of the redeemed person God has destined us to become.

The thorn that continually gnaws at you is a constant reminder that you have unrealistic expectations for yourself, and perhaps of others–that you don't perceive the exalted good of yourself and who God created you to be.

You and I want the thorn to be removed NOW. Yet, God in His infinite wisdom allows it to remain in hopes that we can be truly healed of our pride and self-importance.

Patience

The thorn gives us the opportunity to grow in patience, allowing God to accomplish mighty works in us.

Therefore, "count it all joy, when you fall into diverse temptations; knowing that the trying of your faith worketh patience. And patience hath a perfect work; that you may be perfect and entire, failing at nothing" (Jm 1:2–4). Your perfection is an exalted good that demands much respect, admiration, and patience with yourself and with God. Your future glory is so great, so important, that God allows the thorn to remain–for the purpose of testing you, purifying you, and perfecting you through patience, so that you may fail at nothing and to ensure that you obtain that promised, cherished glory. Be patient with yourself. . . . God is infinitely patient with you.

Effect #3:

Perseverance

Quitter. The very word reeks with contempt. As the saying goes, "nobody likes a quitter." The definition of a quitter is "a person who gives up easily or does not have the courage or determination to finish a task." Considering this, what, in the final analysis, causes someone to quit?

Nearly two decades ago, I was diagnosed with cancer. Feeling defeated, I shared the diagnosis with a friend–a kind of second mom, a woman in her seventies–saying presumptuously, "Well I guess I get to go to heaven." As fast as lightning she sailed into me, "Oh no you don't! You have that beautiful wife and those beautiful children to care for. You don't get off that easy! You have a job to do. You must fight to live! You must fight for them!" Ouch. I couldn't even get a loveable old lady to feel sorry for me. Nobody, not even seventy-year-old sweet mommy-like women, likes quitters.

The quitter is plagued with and battered by discouragement, which bites at and consumes his determination. Discouragement (anti-courage) is always linked to, if not born from, some type of doubt–usually rooted in some type of deception.

In nearly every area of my life—marriage, occupation, faith, remodeling projects, friendships, finances, physical health, familial relationships, entrepreneurial initiatives, personal projects, business partners, collaboration with contractors—I've felt the intense urge, at one time or another, to quit.

When things become difficult, we hear that cunning, seductive, deceptive appeal to "just give up," "surrender," "it's too difficult," or "it's simply not worth it." But ultimately, all those doubts come down to: "what difference does it really make?" The answer is a lot. If you persevere in little matters, you will be entrusted with larger more significant matters; if you quit in small matters, you will never accomplish anything substantial, let alone small.

If doubt causes discouragement, and discouragement instills a lack of determination, and lack of determination leads to quitting, then it appears that the key to stopping the process is never allowing it to start–with doubt.

Why do we doubt? Adversity causes pain; and that pain begins to eclipse our desire to aspire–to press on courageously with hope.

This brings us to the foundational reason we give up, surrender, or quit: the suffering seems to outweigh the desirable goal. In other words, "You've got to want it." If you don't want "it," you won't suffer for "it."

Before proceeding, it is important to clarify what "it" is. Ultimately, "it" comes down to this: a person suffers for what he loves and hopes to obtain what he loves. The two motivational factors are love and hope. Self-help gurus work tirelessly to convince us that we simply need to "do it" or "will it," but ultimately you cannot will it if there is no love in it. You won't do it if 'it' doesn't give you hope.

It has been said, "Don't love something that can't love you back." But self-helpers are experts at convincing us to love something that can't love us back: money, autonomy, a financial enterprise, personal magnetism. Yet none of those things can love us in return. Self-helpers use the bait and switch tactic. They convince people that they can obtain "it," and suffer for "it," because "it" will make us love ourselves, which will make us happy. Self-helpers groom self-lovers, and self-lovers often become self-haters who struggle to love themselves, and therefore struggle to love anyone else. Time after time obtaining "it," leaves the person miserable. Why? Because "it," can't love them in return; because "it" doesn't help them love themselves truly; and because "it" doesn't make others love them for who they really are.

It is a tremendous challenge to press on in the face of adversity: to get turned down for a job and yet continue to apply; to be rejected, yet ask another woman out on a date; to fail at a project, yet persevere; to be in a strained relationship, yet remain lovingly present; to be persecuted, yet remain faithful to your Lord Jesus Christ.

How do people overcome the overwhelming temptation to quit? How do people step up, in the face of adversity, and become better, become the person they were made to be? A clue exists in St. Paul's words, which initially may scandalize us: "more than that, we rejoice in our sufferings, knowing that suffering produces endurance, and endurance produces character, and character produces hope, and hope does not disappoint us, because God's love has been poured into our hearts through the Holy Spirit who has been given to us" (Rom 5:3–5).

Rejoice in sufferings? How can that be?

We will encounter daily a plethora of duties, obligations, and relational situations that cause us suffering. How do we persevere in such situations? What is the secret to, as St. Paul says, "rejoice in suffering"?

Perseverance

First, it is vital that we understand that peace and fulfillment are not the result of having no problems. Peace and fulfillment are born from being resolute in hope.

Second, it is imperative to understand what we are hoping for. This is the "it" that we referred to earlier. If you're hoping to obtain what you do not love, and then you encounter adversity, obstacles, and suffering in your attempt to attain "it," you will likely surrender the cause.

Suffering produces endurance; endurance produces character; those with character are filled with hope, and we hope for that which we love.

What then is the secret to remaining motivated by things that do not motivate you? How can a person be willing to suffer for things that cause him suffering? How does a person persevere when he feels the overwhelming urge to give up?

The one who perseveres is the one who wants or loves the object of his desire so intensely that he will embrace the means, the suffering, and the adversity–using them for his advantage. He uses that what he doesn't love to attain what he loves.

According to St. Thomas Aquinas, "A person who hopes for something strives eagerly to endure all kinds of difficulty and distress. Thus, for example, a sick person, if he wants to become healthy, is happy to take the bitter medicine which will cure him. Therefore, one sign of the ardent hope that is ours thanks to Christ is that we glory not only in the hope of future glory, but also in the afflictions we suffer in order to attain it."[1]

A man may disdain washing dishes, but because he loves his wife, he learns to love scrubbing pots and pans.

---

1 Navarre Bible Commentary, Romans; p 96

Perseverance

No martyr loves execution, or the instrument of torture, yet because of his great love for Christ, he embraces his cross and embraces his execution.

When "God's love has been poured into our hearts," when "the Holy Spirit has been given to us," we are willing to persevere in the face of great sufferings because we are certain that these sufferings are not in vain, but are for the One we love, and in hope of attaining union with the God we love. This is our undying hope–this is the "it."

It is difficult to trust someone who doesn't suffer well. In fact, we laud those who have suffered for a just cause. No one lauds the slothful, jobless, dope-smoking, mid-twenties male who lives in his parent's basement. Why? Because he isn't worthy of following. His life lacks heroism and character, because heroism and character are born from perseverance.

The Thorn

We respect the soldiers who, in the face of eminent death, stormed Normandy beach, many forfeiting their lives to ensure that humanity could be free of Hitler and his regime. We respect such men because, in spite of tremendous suffering, they persevered in hope for a noble purpose. These men had tremendous character.

We all need to learn how to persevere, especially when we don't feel like it; and that is precisely why the thorn remains. The sting of the thorn discourages us and tempts us to surrender the cause. Yet, God allows your thorn to remain for the purpose of teaching you how to persevere, especially, when it appears to be too difficult. The sting of the thorn reminds us to persevere even in the midst of adversity, apparent failure, and suffering.

Remember, "Suffering produces endurance and endurance produces character, and character produces hope" (See Rom 5:3).

Perseverance

The thorn is like a spur with which God figuratively "kicks us," reminding us to "giddy-up!" and ride on in courageous hope toward the goal: God, whom we love. When we use the thorn in this way, we learn to persevere, and that perseverance accomplishes something incredible in us: it makes us people of character, worthy of the allegiance of others and fellowship with God, because we never lose hope in Him.

Effect #4:

Mercy

The critic criticizes others; a judgmental person judges persons; the accuser accuses; and the self-righteous person believes himself to be right.

We, being the victims of such pharisaical elitists, believe ourselves justified and just even as we criticize the critic for being critical, as we accuse the accuser of accusing, and as we condemn the one who condemns us. By doing this we prove one thing: that we are no less guilty than they are.

The Thorn

Recently I received an unsolicited email advising me, "You need to . . ." To which I was immediately tempted to reply, "You need to stop telling people what they need to do!" Guilty as charged.

People often are critical of people they envy, or condemning of those with whom they disagree. The condemnation and criticism stem from a form of resentment that is lodged deep within the soul, seething and simmering, eventually coming to a boil, spilling over in the mess of slander, harsh assessments, demeaning remarks, biting calumnies, marginalizing of others, retaliation, and vengeance.

What is the common trait of the critic, the self-righteous, the elitist, the accuser, and the one who condemns? Each of them lacks compassion and is nearly bankrupt of mercy.

You may fear an elitist's power and influence, but

you'll struggle to love him. You may temporarily placate a critic with your "due respect," believing him to be your ally, until the day he disrespects you. Ultimately, people don't love and respect the accuser, the critic, or the self-righteous elitist who condemns. But they do fear such a person. We fear and endure the micro-managing employer who criticizes our every decision. We dread the elitist critic who will be publishing a review of our latest manuscript.

This is the reason why half of the world hates Christ, and the other half really loves Him: because half of the world believes him to be a tyrannical, overbearing, rule-mongering judge who accuses and condemns people for the slightest infraction; while the other half are attracted to Him precisely for His infinite mercy.

The elitist remains above, perceiving all things from his ivory tower, while God, who actually is elite, understands our plight because He chose to physically experience our frail, pathetic condition. He lowered Himself to our level and extends compassion and mercy for the purpose of lifting us up to heaven. He did not come to the world to condemn it, but to save it. By taking on our human nature, not just for an earthly lifetime, but for all eternity, He continually sees us in himself, and He sees Himself in us; and having this vision of us, He chooses not to condemn us, but forgive us.

Yet, this unconditional love has a stipulation: that we be as merciful as He is merciful. There may be no more important Christian theme than the golden rule. Judge not and you will not be judged. Forgive and you will be forgiven. Give and you will receive. The merciful will receive mercy. But if you condemn, you will be condemned; if you judge, you will be judged. The most well-known stories in the history of man–The

Prodigal Son and The Good Samaritan–demonstrate this rule winsomely.

Only God can condemn a person; yet, He has gone out of His way to show by His very self-sacrifice that He would rather not have to. A sinner cannot judge another sinner's soul. No sinner can make a just judgment of another because his vision is clouded by his own personal sin.

Additionally, a saint won't judge a sinner because he loves the sinner and believes himself to be one. As St. Teresa of Calcutta noted, "If you judge people, you have no time to love them." Often, we condemn others for the iniquity we perceive in ourselves–or more precisely, we condemn others for what we refuse to acknowledge about ourselves.

Recently, I listened to a man rant for over an hour about a man who ranted for an hour during a meeting he had chaired. Later, I ranted to my wife about my meeting with this man who consumed our meeting with his ranting. We blindly condemn others for that which we are guilty. This is why the thorn remains.

The thorn is a warning signal that we aren't perfect; that in fact, we are weak; that we struggle and have to muster our strength to overcome evil, sin, and temptation–and even then, it may not be enough.

The thorn helps to convict you that you are one of them, that you are a sinner in need of mercy. The thorn gives us a window through which we can perceive, and relate to, the miserable condition and plight of others, because we have our own miserable plight.

When the sting of the thorn is absent, it is easy to believe ourselves better than others. Suddenly the thorn pricks at you, demanding that you remember the dirt from which you came. You and I, and all of humanity, were born in sin, are sinners, and suffer from the same loathsome condition. Yet, God is patiently merciful, offfering his consolation to us amidst our most vicious struggles. As St. Paul says, "Blessed be the God and Father of our Lord Jesus Christ, the Father of mercies, and the God of all comfort, who comforts us in all our tribulations; that we may be able to comfort them who are in all distress, by the exhortation wherewith we are also exhorted by God" (2 Cor 1:3–4).

God comforts us while we endure our own distressing thorn, that we may be inspired to comfort others in the way we have been comforted. This is one of the powerful benefits of the thorn: it helps you to stop condemning and begin forgiving–from the heart.

The exhortation of God is to, "forgive one another in Christ, even as God in Christ has forgiven you." We pray often, "Forgive us our trespasses as we have forgiven those who trespass against us." Ask yourself, "*How* have I forgiven those who have sinned against me?" Have I forgiven from my heart? The level and manner with which we forgive others, we are asking God to apply to us.

The thorn gently reminds us that we are in desperate need of divine mercy; and that without God's forgiveness, we are helpless wretches doomed for eternal death. The thorn exists to remind you that the mercy you have received from God, you must in turn give to others to avoid that wretched death. God may not remove your thorn until this type of mercy reigns in your heart. Yet, the good news is that your thorn, if embraced properly, will aid you in receiving God's mercy and becoming merciful like God.

Effect #5:

Humility

Most of us have experienced that awkward, alarming, shameful, moment when after meeting with someone we discover that we had toothpaste residue plastered on our upper lip, a zipper down, a black peppercorn wedged between a couple of our front teeth, a dry booger magically suspended at the opening of one of our nostrils. Upon realization, several sentiments simultaneously crash upon our ego:

The Thorn

First, "How did I miss that? It's so obvious!" Second, "I can't take it back; no control Z; no rewind; the moment is irrevocable." Third, "There may be hope . . . what if they didn't see it . . . they didn't say anything . . . that's good. If they saw it they would have said something." Fourth, "You didn't say anything when your buddy Bill had that smeared chocolate chip on the side of his face that looked like dog ----- Ugh."

Similarly, regardless as to how blind we might be to our own pride, others easily perceive it. It has been said that pride is like bad breath: everyone knows you have it but you.

Pride is the enemy inside. It's the unidentifiable cancer that has infected the entire soul. Pride is cunning and difficult to perceive because it leaches itself to a person—from its earliest days—pretending to be a part of that person.

Humility

In fact, over the years of a person's existence, pride disguises itself as something good such as honor, self-respect, dignity, an unwillingness to compromise, a show of strength; a demonstration of fool-hearty courage; a relentless will. It is like a spiritual chameleon that takes on any fundamental attribute that at first glance appears honorable, but usually in the end shows itself to be nothing more than an unhealthy coping mechanism that helps us ignore or avoid humiliations.

C.S. Lewis said that "Pride is spiritual cancer: it eats up every possibility of love, or contentment, or common sense." "Pride is the primal sin, and most grave of all the sins, the spiritual rebellion that unturned the harmony of the universe. Pride is also the most glamorous, pervasive, fatal, and insidious of the sins. The saints have to be on guard as they develop, not to take pride in their own virtue and the grace they have received lest all be turned to evil, and they follow Lucifer in fall from bright to dark."[2]

Pride is the most insidious and pervasive of sins because, as the word demonstrates, "I" is at the center of P R I D E. Your most contentious enemy is not God, the devil, or your mother-in-law–it's pride.

Pride has been defined as the excessive love of one's own excellence. Because of love of his own self worth, the creature withdraws itself from subjection to Almighty God. He thinks himself to be above God's commands and above the commands of his superior. Pride is rated as one of the blackest sins because the creature, in his self-exaltation, refuses to submit.[3] Pride is the root-ball from which all other sins grow.

Pride in Latin is *superbia,* because a man attempts

---

2   Wisdom of the Saint; Jill Hack Adels
3   See NewAdvent.org; Pride

to aim higher (supra) than he is. A man is proud who wishes to appear above (supra) what he really is. "For he who wishes to overstep beyond what he is, is proud."[4] In other words, in an effort to appear "above" others, the person refuses to be "below" anyone. Consider the devil's dictum, "non servium (I will not serve)," as opposed to Christ's, "I did not come to be served, but to serve . . ." Which of the two do you think suffers from pride?

The consequence of pride is that a person becomes stupid, because they are unwilling to humble themselves below another for the purpose of learning from another; they remain stuck in their worldview because they are unwilling to follow others; they are reduced to pettiness because they cannot acknowledge greatness in others. Pride destroys a person's ability to admire,

4   St. Thomas Aquinas

follow, and collaborate with others. Such a person rejects others' knowledge, gifts, authority, and superiority in the effort to maintain a false self-understanding of itself as greater than others. The person bound by pride stunts his own personal growth, because he believes that his way is best and that there is no need to look to others for counsel–because to do so would indicate that he is not above everyone else.

We all wrestle with pride, or at least we should. If you aren't striving to overcome pride; pride has already overcome you. And don't go to the other extreme of believing you are the most prideful person in the world–that type of false humility simply proves that you are prideful.

If we are to grow spiritually and become saints, it is essential that pride be rooted out from our souls and replaced with humility, which is the foundation of all the virtues. Yet, God does not force or coerce any individual. God respects the human person's free will to choose his own fate. Yet, God uses humiliations as a way to humble us, and awake us from our prideful stupor. St. Francis de Sales pointedly remarked that "The path to humility is paved with the sharp stones of humiliations."

St. Thomas explains that God sometimes permits certain kinds of evil in order to draw out greater good: for example, in order to protect people from pride–the root of all vices–He sometimes allows his chosen ones to be humiliated by an illness, or a defect, or even a mortal sin, in order that the person who is humbled in this way might recognize that he cannot stand firm by his own efforts alone. Hence it is said in Romans 8:28, "We know that in everything God works for good with those who love him"–not of course that

God seeks the sin but [the sinner's] turning to him."[5]

If humility is the foundational attribute of every saint, and if this virtue is obtained by humiliations, your thorn is a great benefit in that it can serve as a remedy for pride.

The thorn is a continual humiliation that causes us to cast aside the idea that we are somehow above anyone, or that we are excellent. Why? Because you and I are not so above others that we don't have a thorn like them, nor are we so excellent that we are capable of removing our own thorn. The only way to remove the thorn is to humble ourselves before the only One who can remove it. Operating from humility, we can use whatever is excellent in us for the service of doing good for others.

Often the thorn remains because we simply think too

---

5   Navarre Bible Commentary 2 Cor

much of ourselves and what we've accomplished. We may exteriorly praise God for His works being accomplished in us, but secretly we pride ourselves taking great personal satisfaction in our achievements–particularly those that others have not accomplished.

"If one glories in some divine gift, as coming from God, that is a good boast, because it is boasting in the Lord. But if one glories in that gift as something coming from oneself, then it is a bad kind of boast."[6]

It has been said that humility is not to think less of oneself, but rather to think of one's self less. The thorn remains to convict us of the fact that we often think too much of ourselves, and about ourselves too much. We give far too much credit to ourselves for those things that God is accomplishing in us. The thorn is proof that

---

6   St. Thomas Aquinas, Navarre p 238; 2 Cor

The Thorn

we are not God, not above sin, not above others, not capable of saving ourselves. We need to be saved.

I often marvel at the irony of the testimonial of a Christian who says, "When I was saved." It sounds humble enough. But upon further examination it becomes evident that "I" is at the center of the statement, and the "Lord," who did all of the saving, is not mentioned. Pride is so deep that we have difficulty admitting that we were saved without our own help.

The thorn exists as a continual reminder that we are not the one who saves; for we cannot save ourselves; only God can accomplish such a deed. Compared to pride, the thorn is the lesser evil, which God can, and will use, to humiliate us in order that we may become humble, and becoming humble, we may become great in Him.

"Let nothing be done through contention, neither by vain glory: but in humility, let each esteem others better

Humility

than themselves" (Phil 2:3). The thorn is a great benefit to us in that it compels us to do just that–count others as better than ourselves.

Effect #6:

Gratefulness

Have you ever made a deal with God? Perhaps you were stuck in a job that was going no where and prayed and begged God for a new start; a new career. If he would provide the job, you would never commit "that" sin again.

Maybe you were desperate for a spouse, someone you could love and someone who really loved you. If God would only answer your prayer, you in turn would be faithful, prayerful, and religious.

It is common for parents, when faced with the strong probability that their in-utero baby could be born with a defect, to implore God, begging Him to provide a miracle, and if that miracle be given, they will dedicate their lives, and the baby's life, in service to Him.

All of us have been there. All of us have made deals with God. Yet, after we received that favor for which we begged, did we remember to thank God–a day later, a week later, a year later?

Typically, we spend our prayer times complaining and griping about the demands of a career that God gave us, or the tensions with the spouse He granted, or the disobedience of that miracle baby who became a perfectly healthy, normal, defiant teen. Adam, who longed for a helper fit for him, was given Eve, who eventually seduced him to sin. When God asked Adam why he had committed the sin, he said, "It was because of the woman whom You put me here with." Notice the implication, Adam blamed God for the blessing God had given.

It's a fairly common dynamic: we beg God for a particular blessing, then we condemn Him for granting it. All too often the solution becomes a problem, and the blessing becomes a curse.

This is a type of spiritual amnesia, a forgetfulness of our personal journey. The many healings, provisions, loosed bonds, and re-forged relationships slip our minds. We allow the daily tensions, responsibilities, duties, and difficulties to grind away at our ability to recognize that God has answered our prayers—even those blessings he provides without our asking.

We pray incessantly, begging, pleading with tears, petitioning for an ease of a dreadful plight, an ailing disorder to be healed, a debilitating situation to be removed, that God would bestow relief. After God performs the mighty work of mercy, which seemed nearly impossible, we progressively forget that the work was mighty or merciful as it becomes yesterday's news.

The Savior's words ring as true today as they did when spoken nearly two thousand years ago: "Were not ten healed? Where are the other nine?"

God is not interested in making a deal. He doesn't want to extract anything from you. The sacrifice He desires is not your money, but the sacrifice of thanksgiving (see Ps 50). This is the sacrifice that He has told us He desires. Why? Because by thanking Him we sacrifice the pride that dupes us into believing that we have obtained what we have by our own power. Because by thanking him, we sacrifice our envy of what others have–and we selfishly wish we could have– and praise

God that we have enough. Saying to God, "Thank you. You have given me more than I deserve," is a sacrifice, because many times we think we deserve more.

Years ago I met a man, who by the world's standards achieved the highest honors in nearly every category. Yet in his retirement, he searched the heavens, begging God for another door, another opportunity that could give him meaning. Professional athlete, All-Conference collegiate football player; COO of not one, but several highly profitable fortune 500 companies; a gorgeous wife; a mountain of money that would endure several lifetimes; beach houses in the most choice locations; best-selling author; father, grandfather; respected in every circle of his fellows as the most successful, talented, capable man they knew. Yet, he wanted more. In his prayers to God, while begging for that second door to open, he heard the divine plea, "Am I not sufficient for you?"

We're all like him. We all suffer from spiritual amnesia. We forget the answered prayers, and therefore forget to be grateful.

Maybe God doesn't grant greater accomplishments because we aren't thankful for the ones He already allowed us to accomplish. Maybe God's power and presence is decreasing because we've neglected to be grateful for His ever-increasing presence in our lives. Maybe that annoying, biting, menacing little thorn remains in us because we've neglected to reflect upon and thank God for the many thorns that He has already removed.

"Take with thee words, and return to the Lord" (Hos 14:2). A most beneficial exercise is to take mental notes of your life's story, and ask God to help you see the many and varied ways He has intervened with His mercy and generosity. Compile that list of favors, and then take that list to prayer and thank God for what He has accomplished in your life.

What thorns has He removed? It could be as simple as the healing of a toothache, the impossible miracle of meeting your spouse, the healing of a friendship, the cure of an addiction, the saving of your life, a new career opportunity, twenty-five years of marriage, a quiet dinner with your spouse. If you reflect with serious attention, your list of things to thank God for will be endless.

If you are thankful for the little things; you will not be concerned about having more things. If you are grateful for those small things in life, your concern will not be obtaining big things. Those who neglect being thankful for what they have, while wanting more, will always have less.

Your thorn is a sweet reminder of those thorns that the divine physician has already removed. Thanks-

The Thorn

giving for those thorns removed eases the restless striving and incessant wanting for more, and replaces this anxious desiring with peace. This peace provides a true joy: the ability to rejoice in God, who doesn't make deals but simply gives, and gives, and gives. And how does He want us to respond to this infinite generosity? He wants us to be thankful to Him. That's why the thorn remains: to remind us that this "is God's will for you: to be thankful in all circumstances" (1 Thes 5:18). If and when we become thankful in all circumstances, the thorn that perplexed us will be the source of tremendous joy.

Effect #7:

Knowledge of God

Why would God allow something to exist that seems to separate us from Himself? Why would God allow something bad to keep us from experiencing the good? Why would God allow the thorn to remain? Ultimately, God allows your thorn to remain because he wants you to know Him. He wants you to understand the depths of the relentless, unstoppable, undying love He has for you.

The Thorn

The basis of every real relationship is trust. If trust does not exist in the relationship, it is not a true relationship. Trust is discovered when a relationship is tested, and nothing tests our relationship with God more acutely than our infidelities and weaknesses, and those are revealed when one is assailed by suffering. Sufferings and setbacks, temptations and trials, can gravely test our relationship with God. Temptation can cause us to question whether God can trust us. Suffering can cause us to question whether we can trust God.

When our relationship with God is tested, either because of our weakness or because of suffering, there are two questions that need to be answered: "Can God be trusted?" And, "Will He receive me back?" Your thorn exists to help you answer both of those questions correctly. Yes, He can be trusted; and yes, He will receive you back–in fact, you may have left Him; but He has never left you. Most of us understand this intellectually, but all of us need to encounter this truth experientially. The thorn is a means by which we can experience this truth in the core of our being.

Our Lord Jesus allowed Himself to be crowned and pierced by thorns. The crown of thorns was made by the Roman soldiers as a way to mock Jesus' kingship, his headship and authority over creation. This is why a crown sits upon a king's head and not his ankle: because the head is the sign of authority.

Jesus, though sinless, allowed Himself to be painfully pierced, pricked, brutally stung by thorns, precisely in that area which symbolizes His authority–His head–as a reminder to us that when our thorn pricks our pride, we have a divine savior who understands our plight.

Our thorn may be in our loins, but it pricks at our pride, at our authority, at our belief that we are above

The Thorn

others. Our Lord allowed His head to be pierced by thorns to demonstrate that though He is the King of kings and above all, He uses His authority to serve, to heal, and to love all. By allowing your thorn to remain, he is hoping that you will choose to be united to Him; to use the authority He has given you to serve, love and heal others.

God allows the thorn to remain to help us learn not to rely on ourselves but on Him, the only One who is truly reliable. Your thorn remains to summon you to trust in the only One who is truly trustworthy. The thorn teaches us to rely on God.

God allows the thorn to remain to help us become patient with our own spiritual progress, with our own limitations and defects–and those of others–because He is eternally patient with us, and wants us to know that. God uses the thorn to help you grow in patience and know that He is always patient with you. The thorn teaches us that God is untiringly patient.

God allows the thorn to remain for the purpose of inspiring us to never, ever, give up on ourselves, or on Him, because He will never give up on us. He uses your thorn to help you grow in perseverance and know that His love always perseveres. The thorn teaches us that God's love is enduring and persevering.

God allows the thorn to remain so that we may experience His tender, limitless mercy; and in turn share this divine mercy with those around us–even our enemies. He uses the thorn to remind us to be merciful to ourselves, for He is ever-merciful toward us. The thorn teaches us that God is limitless in his mercy.

God allows the thorn to endure that we may be humiliated, our pride broken, to ensure that we become humble. He uses the thorn to help us become like Him,

The Thorn

who humbled himself, coming in human likeness, becoming a slave, becoming obedient unto death, even death on a cross, and therefore, God highly exalted Him (see Phil 2:6–11). God uses the thorn to humble us, and eventually exalt us in Him. The thorn teaches us that God has made Himself to be most humble for the purpose of exalting us.

God allows the thorn to remain to inspire us to be grateful that He is a God who is patient, His love is persevering. His mercy is endless. And He humbled Himself to show us that humility is the only path to exaltation. He humbled Himself to become one of us, and one with us that we may become one with Him. We can always entrust ourselves to God who has entrusted Himself to us. God allows the thorn to remain to ensure that we can know who God is truly: rich in mercy, generous in love, faithful to the end.

Accepting our thorn does not in any way mean that we can stop fighting against temptation and the tendency toward sin. Accepting our thorn simply means that we stop fighting on our own, and stop hating ourselves when our efforts fail. Remember: self-reliance leads to self-hatred. The thorn alerts us to the truth that God is ready to help the helpless and give us His strength in our weakness.

The world's version of the Gospel tells us that God's strength is demonstrated in our strength and therefore, we must put our strength on display. When we think like the world, we are inclined to put our wealth, our muscles, our achievements, our house, our fans and followers, our beauty, you name it, on display for the world, convincing ourselves all the while that we are glorifying God. But God did not say, "My strength is made perfect in your strength." He said that His strength is made perfect in our weakness.

The Blessed Virgin said that she was the handmaid of the Lord. This is another way of saying that she understood her position in relation to God as a poor, lowly, servant. Yet, she also says, in the same breath, my soul magnifies the Lord. The Lord's greatness is manifested in her lowliness.

God's glory was not ultimately manifested by enslaving populaces of peoples to be His followers, to make them build Him an expansive kingdom. His glory was manifest in His crucifixion, in His most shameful moment. "When the Son of Man is lifted up He will be glorified" (see Jn 12:24).

The irony of the Gospel is that it is not for those who are perfect. Jesus didn't come for those who are perfect. . . . because the perfect don't exist, except in their own self-inflated minds. Christ came not for the righteous, but for the sinner–for me and for you–and that is the best news. The thorn exists to remind us that we are not righteous, but rather, we are sinners; and God loves to manifest His glory in the weakness of sinners who are striving to follow Him.

Like a little child who, when reprimanded for doing something wrong, becomes so alarmed and shocked by his parent's disappointment, he runs to his parent and buries his head in his dad or mom's embrace. Similarly, the thorn compels us to run into the embrace of our loving Father who runs out to meet us. Use your thorn to rest, trustingly, in His embrace, knowing that He loves the sinner. He loves you.

Let us give praise to God, thanking Him for our thorn, for its biting presence is constant proof that His love is relentless, stronger than death. For where sin abounds, grace abounds all the more (see Rom 5:20).